Have Yourself a Sweary Little Christmas

A Sweary Holiday Coloring Book for Adults

FREE DOWNLOAD
KNOB Jockey
FUCKWIT
Shit OUCH
www.honeybadgercoloring.com/christmas
YOUR DOWNLOAD CODE: XMAS335
@honeybadgercoloring
Honey Badger Coloring

Merry
Fucking
Christmas

BITE ME

I PUT
OUT
FOR SANTA

Festive
As Fuck

merry christmas
melf
merry christmas

HO
FUCKITY
HO

MERRY DRUNK!
I'm Christmas!

LIGHT THAT
SHIT UP!

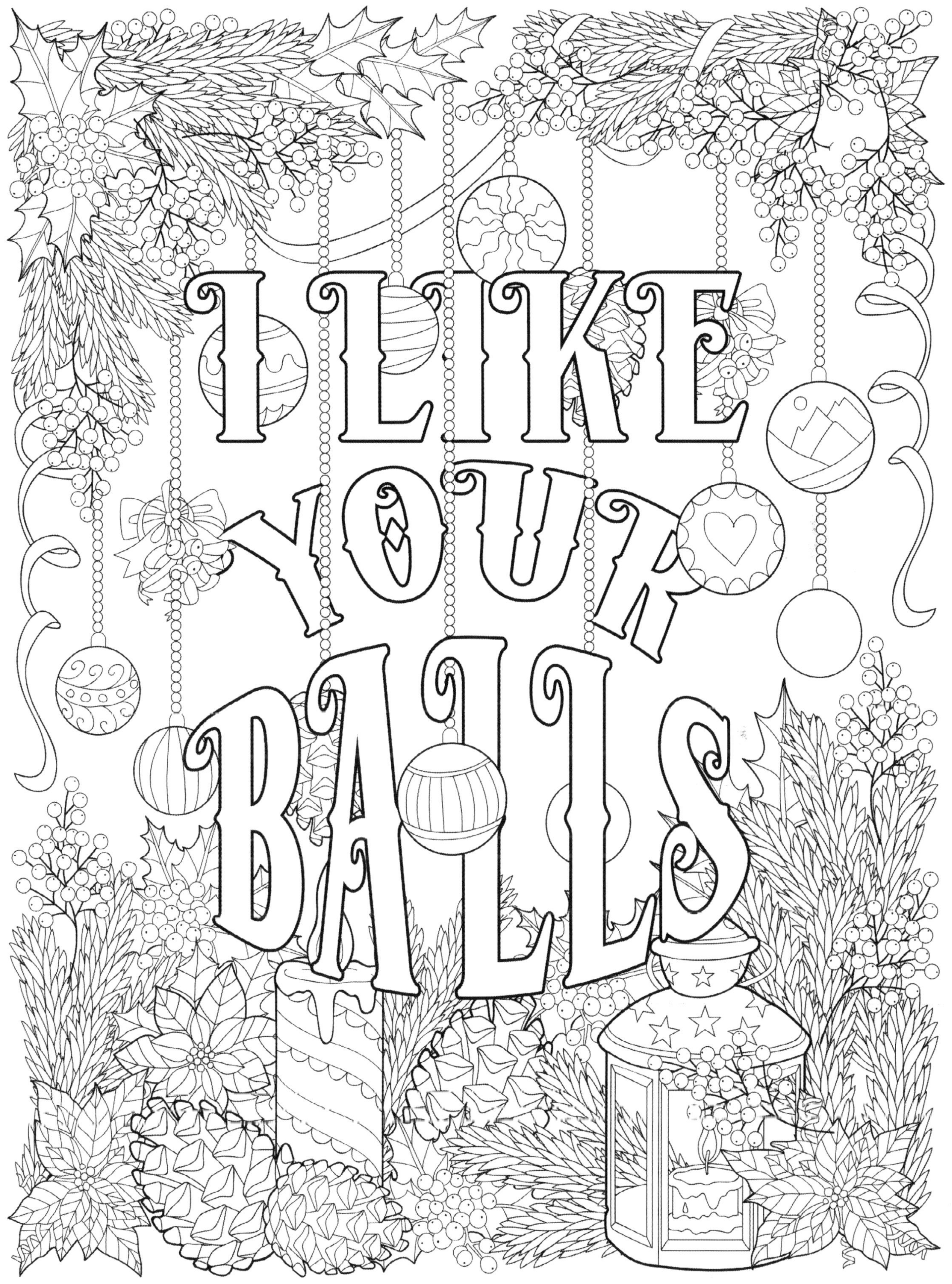

I LIKE
YOUR
BALLS

BAAAA
FUCKING HUMBUG

Merry
Christmas
ASSHOLE!

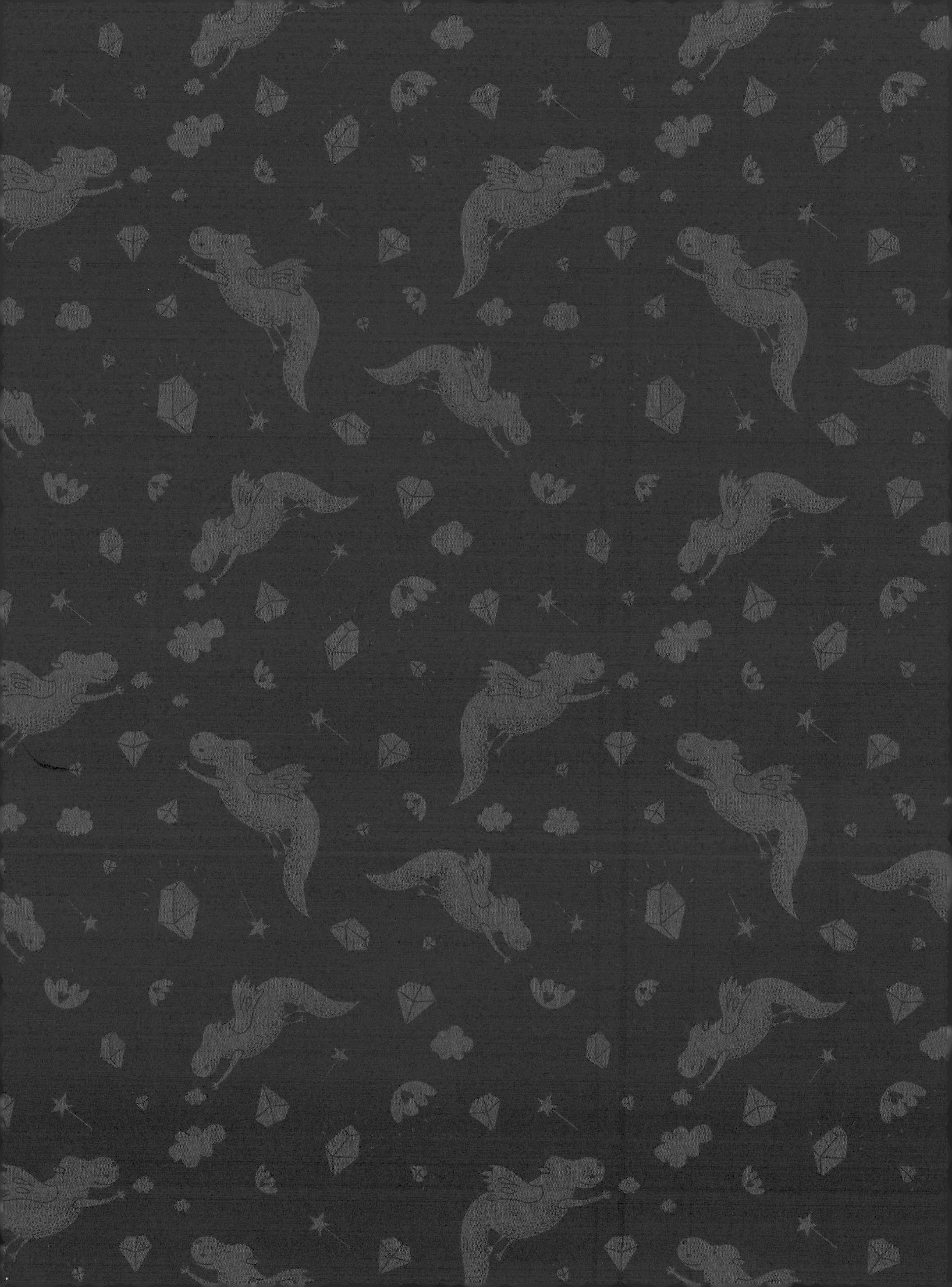

Merry Christmas!
SHITTER WAS FULL!

MERRY CHRISTMAS
Just kidding.
GO FUCK YOURSELF

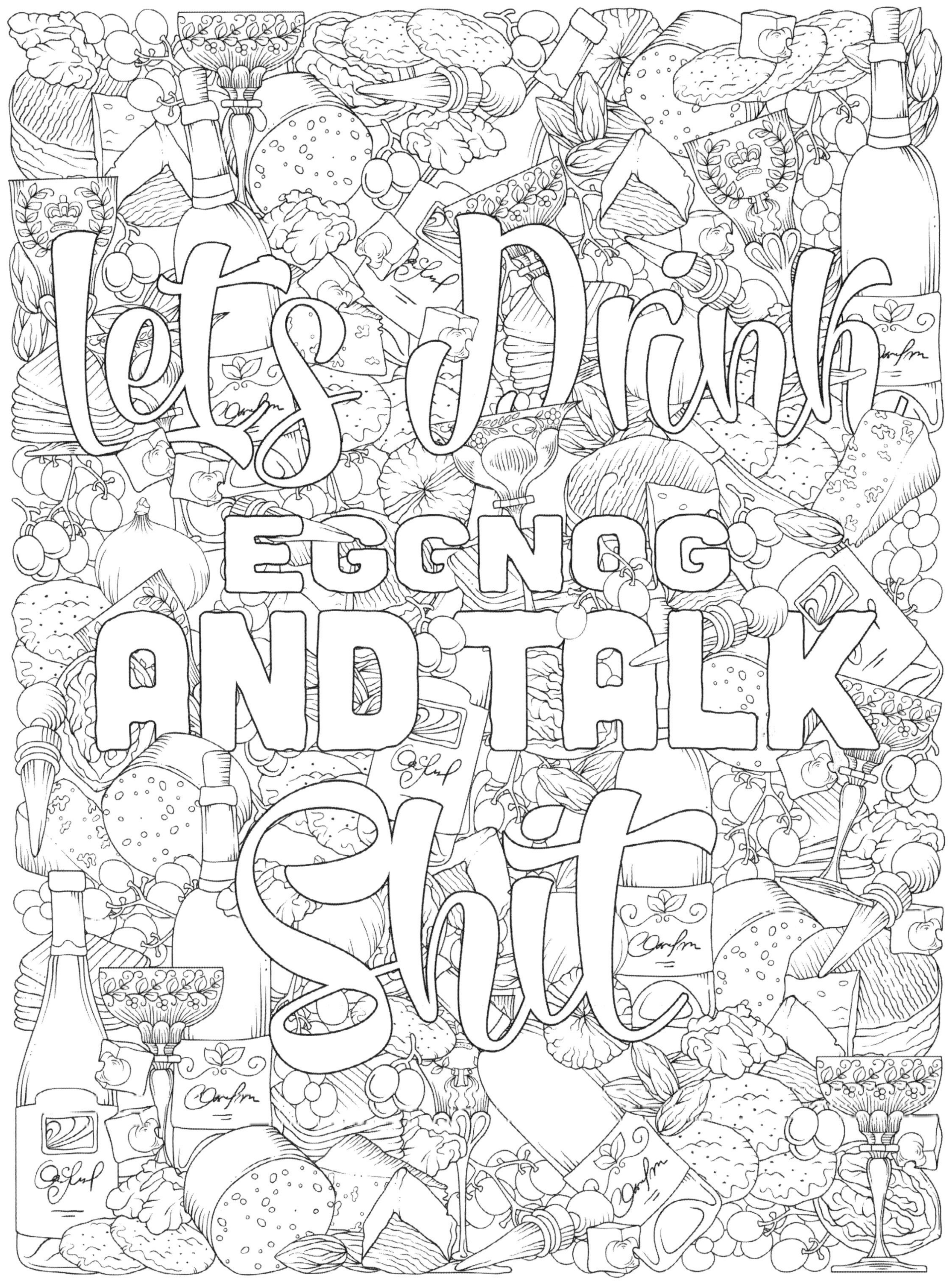

Let's Drink
EGGNOG
AND TALK
Shit

HOLY SHIT!
It's christmas!

HO HO HO,
MOFO!

HUNG LIKE A STOCKING

MERRY CHRISTMAS
BITCH

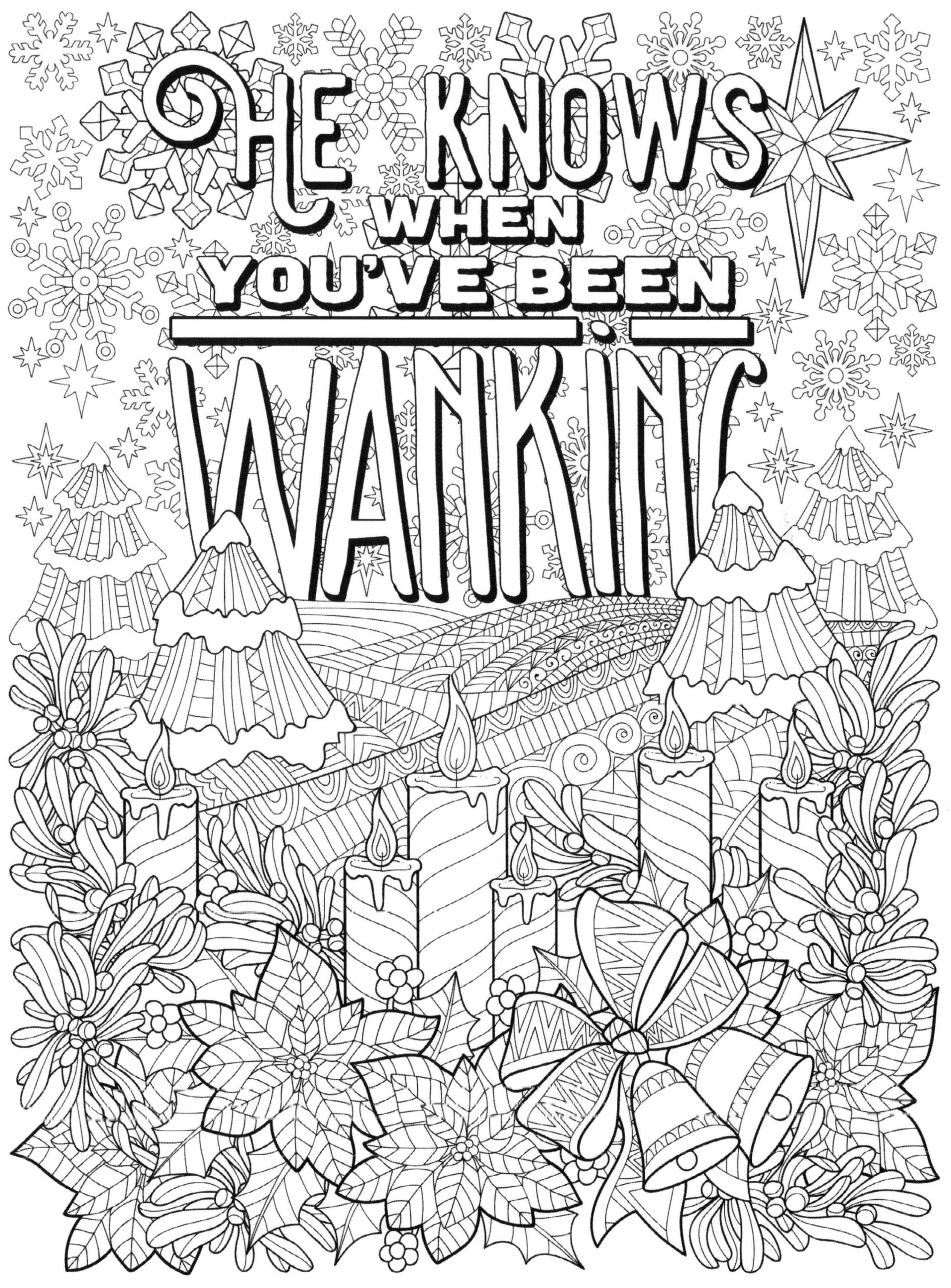

HE KNOWS
WHEN
YOU'VE BEEN
WANKING

Merry Christmas
YOU PRICK

JOLLY AF

Ho Ho Holy
Shit
I'M HUNGOVER

WHATS
IN YOUR
STOCKING?

WISHING YOU
A SHITLOAD
of happiness
THIS HOLIDAY
SEASON

Merry Christmas
Ye olde
CUNT!

Stop Dreaming
OF A WHITE CHRISTMAS
YOU MASSIVE
RACIST!

YOU'RE GETTING
FUCK ALL
FROM SANTA

Back the
Fuck up
BITCH!

MERRY CHRIST-
— LET'S GET FUCKED UP FOR THE WHOLE OF DECEMBER —
-MAS

Ho FUCKING Ho!

CHECK OUT OUR OTHER BOOKS!

www.honeybadgercoloring.com

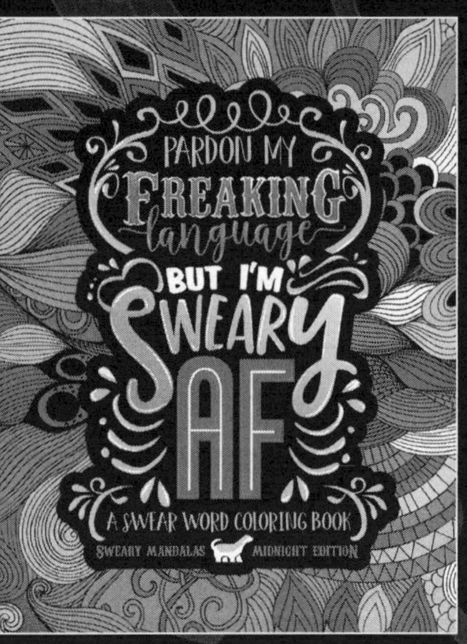

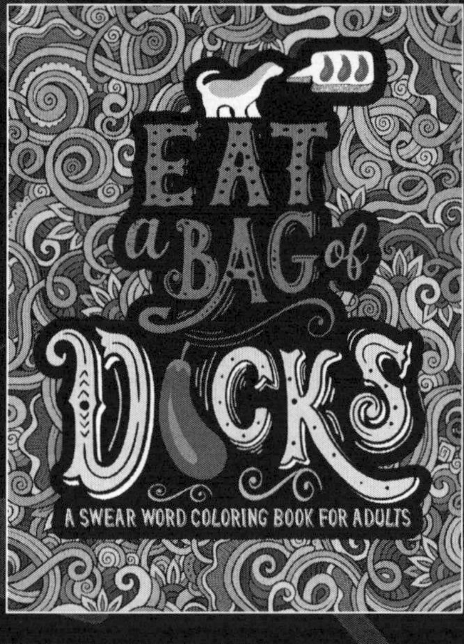

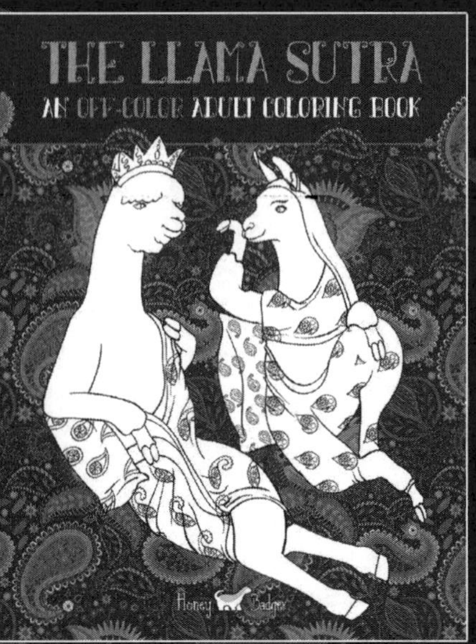

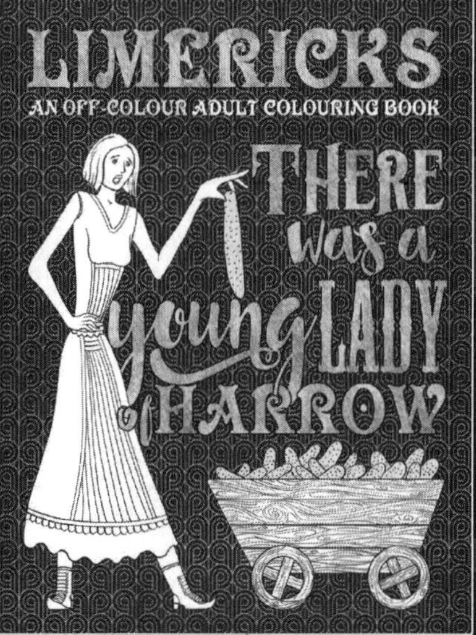

Printed in Great Britain
by Amazon